FAMOUS ATHLETES

JONATHAN TOEWS

by Tracy Nelson Maurer

Gail Saunders-Smith, PhD, Consulting Editor

Pebble Plus

CAPSTONE PRESS
a capstone imprint

Pebble Plus is published by Capstone Press,
1710 Roe Crest Drive, North Mankato, Minnesota 56003
www.capstonepub.com

Library of Congress Cataloging-in-Publication Data
Maurer, Tracy, 1965–
  Jonathan Toews / by Tracy Nelson Maurer.
    pages cm.   (Pebble Plus. Famous Athletes.)
  Includes bibliographical references and index.
  Audience: Age: 5–7.
  Audience: Grade: K to Grade 3.
  ISBN 978-1-4914-6235-5 (library binding)—ISBN 978-1-4914-6251-5 (ebook pdf)—
ISBN 978-1-4914-6255-3 (Pebble Books paperback)
  1. Toews, Jonathan, 1988– —Juvenile literature. 2. Hockey players—United States—
Biography—Juvenile literature. I. Title.
  GV848.5.T64M38 2016
  796.962092—dc23
  [B]   2015001861

Editorial Credits
Erika L. Shores, editor; Juliette Peters, designer; Eric Gohl, media researcher;
Lori Barbeau, production specialist

Photo Credits
Alamy: All Canada Photos, 7; Courtesy of Shattuck-St. Mary's: 9; Dreamstime: Jerry Coli, 1, 22; Getty Images: Bruce Bennett, 15, Elsa, 11; Newscom: Cal Sport Media/Mike Wulf, cover, 21, Icon Sportswire/Robin Alam, 5, MCT/Charles Cherney, 13, Reuters/Brian Snyder, 17, Reuters/Jeff Haynes, 19

Design Elements: Shutterstock

Note to Parents and Teachers

The Famous Athletes set supports national curriculum standards for social studies related to people, places, and culture. This book describes and illustrates Jonathan Toews. The images support early readers in understanding the text. The repetition of words and phrases helps early readers learn new words. This book also introduces early readers to subject-specific vocabulary words, which are defined in the Glossary section. Early readers may need assistance to read some words and to use the Table of Contents, Glossary, Read More, Internet Sites, Critical Thinking Using the Common Core, and Index sections of the book.

Printed in the United States of America in North Mankato, Minnesota.
042015   008823CGF15

TABLE OF CONTENTS

SKATING STAR

NHL star Jonathan Bryan Toews

was born April 29, 1988.

His father, Bryan, first strapped

ice skates on Jonathan at age 3.

By age 5 Jonathan was

a very good skater.

NHL stands for National Hockey League.

Say Toews: TAYVZ

1988

born in
Winnipeg,
Manitoba

Jonathan loved playing outdoors in Canada. In winter his parents built a backyard ice rink. Jonathan and his brother, David, played ice hockey for hours.

1988

born in
Winnipeg,
Manitoba

Children skate on an outdoor ice rink.

At age 15 Jonathan left Canada to go to Shattuck-St. Mary's in Minnesota. The high school's hockey team has won many championships. Jonathan's team won in 2005.

1988

born in
Winnipeg,
Manitoba

2003–
2005

attends
Shattuck-
St. Mary's
School

After high school Jonathan went

to college in North Dakota.

He led the school's hockey team

to the national playoffs in 2006

and 2007.

1988

born in
Winnipeg,
Manitoba

2003–2005

attends
Shattuck-
St. Mary's
School

2005–2007

attends
University
of North
Dakota

NHL SUPERSTAR

The Chicago Blackhawks chose

Jonathan in the 2006 NHL Draft.

He joined the team the next year.

He was 19. He scored his first

NHL goal on his first shot

in his first game!

1988
born in Winnipeg, Manitoba

2003–2005
attends Shattuck-St. Mary's School

2005–2007
attends University of North Dakota

2006
signs with the Chicago Blackhawks

Jonathan shined as the team's center. He was a leader on the ice. The Blackhawks made him team captain in 2008. In 2010 he helped the team win the Stanley Cup.

1988 — born in Winnipeg, Manitoba

2003–2005 — attends Shattuck-St. Mary's School

2005–2007 — attends University of North Dakota

2006 — signs with the Chicago Blackhawks

2008 — becomes team captain at age 20

2010 — helps the Blackhawks win first Stanley Cup since 1961

Jonathan earned a spot on Canada's Olympic hockey team in 2010. His team won the gold medal. In 2014 Jonathan and Team Canada won the gold medal again.

1988 born in Winnipeg, Manitoba

2003–2005 attends Shattuck-St. Mary's School

2005–2007 attends University of North Dakota

2006 signs with the Chicago Blackhawks

2008 becomes team captain at age 20

2010 helps the Blackhawks win first Stanley Cup since 1961

2010 wins Olympic gold medal

Jonathan and the Blackhawks won

the Stanley Cup again in 2013.

The next season the Blackhawks

tried to win back-to-back titles.

But they lost in the semifinals.

1988	2003– 2005	2005– 2007	2006	2008	2010	2010	2013	2014
born in Winnipeg, Manitoba	attends Shattuck- St. Mary's School	attends University of North Dakota	signs with the Chicago Blackhawks	becomes team captain at age 20	helps the Blackhawks win first Stanley Cup since 1961	wins Olympic gold medal	helps the Blackhawks win the Stanley Cup	wins Olympic gold medal

LOOKING AHEAD

In 2015 Jonathan led his team
to another Stanley Cup.
He has led winning teams
ever since he learned to skate.
Jonathan plans to help his team
win for many more seasons.

1988	2003–2005	2005–2007	2006	2008	2010	2010	2013	2014	2015
born in Winnipeg, Manitoba	attends Shattuck-St. Mary's School	attends University of North Dakota	signs with the Chicago Blackhawks	becomes team captain at age 20	helps the Blackhawks win first Stanley Cup since 1961	wins Olympic gold medal	helps the Blackhawks win the Stanley Cup	wins Olympic gold medal	helps the Blackhawks win the Stanley Cup

Jonathan Toews

GLOSSARY

back-to-back—two in a row

captain—the player on the team who is the leader; the captain wears the letter "C" on his jersey

center—a skater who mainly plays in the middle of the ice

draft—an event held for teams to choose new people to play for them

season—the time of year in which NHL hockey games are played

semifinal—the round of games that decides which team goes on to compete for the championship

Stanley Cup—the trophy given to the team that wins the NHL championship

title—the championship of a league

READ MORE

Doeden, Matt. *Stars of Hockey.* Sports Stars. North Mankato, Minn.: Capstone Press, 2014.

Durrie, Karren. *Hockey.* Let's Play. New York: AV2 by Weigl, 2012.

Rausch, David. *National Hockey League.* Epic: Major League Sports. Minneapolis: Bellwether Media, Inc., 2014.

INTERNET SITES

FactHound offers a safe, fun way to find Internet sites related to this book. All of the sites on FactHound have been researched by our staff.

Here's all you do:

Visit *www.facthound.com*

Type in this code: 9781491462355

Super-cool stuff!

Check out projects, games and lots more at
www.capstonekids.com

CRITICAL THINKING USING THE COMMON CORE

1. Jonathan had a backyard ice rink as a child. How might this have helped him become a good hockey player? (Integration of Knowledge and Ideas)

2. Read the text on page 14. Then look at the photograph on page 15. What is Jonathan holding? (Craft and Structure)

INDEX

Word Count: 259
Grade: 1
Early-Intervention Level: 18